It's
ALWAYS
BEER
O'CLOCK

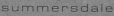

summersdale

IT'S ALWAYS BEER O'CLOCK

First published in 2015
This edition copyright © Summersdale Publishers Ltd, 2017

Images © Shutterstock

Summersdale Publishers Ltd
46 West Street
Chichester
West Sussex
PO19 1RP
UK

www.summersdale.com

Printed and bound in the Czech Republic

ISBN: 978-1-78685-008-9

Substantial discounts on bulk quantities of Summersdale books are available to corporations, professional associations and other organisations. For details contact general enquiries: telephone: +44 (0) 1243 771107, fax: +44 (0) 1243 786300 or email: enquiries@summersdale.com.

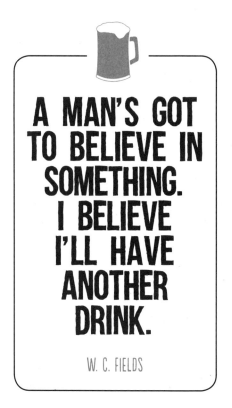

A MAN'S GOT
TO BELIEVE IN
SOMETHING.
I BELIEVE
I'LL HAVE
ANOTHER
DRINK.

W. C. FIELDS

BEER SEEMS
LIKE AN EVEN
BETTER IDEA
AFTER YOU'VE
HAD SOME BEER.

STEVEN HALL

GOD HAS A
BROWN VOICE,
AS SOFT AND
FULL AS BEER.

ANNE SEXTON

GOOD
PEOPLE
DRINK
GOOD
BEER.

HUNTER S. THOMPSON

COME, LANDLORD, FILL A FLOWING BOWL UNTIL IT DOES RUN OVER; TONIGHT WE WILL ALL MERRY BE – TOMORROW WE'LL GET SOBER.

JOHN FLETCHER

Fermentation equals civilisation.

John Ciardi

—

STAY WITH THE
BEER. BEER IS
CONTINUOUS BLOOD.
A CONTINUOUS LOVER.

—

CHARLES BUKOWSKI

ALL IS
FAIR
— *in* —
LOVE AND
BEER.

ANONYMOUS

The drink you like the best
should be the drink you
drink the most.

J. B. BURGESS

Nothing ever tasted better
than a cold beer on a
beautiful afternoon with
nothing to look forward to
than more of the same.

HUGH HOOD

WHEN I DRINK, I THINK; AND WHEN I THINK, I DRINK.

FRANÇOIS RABELAIS

NO SOLDIER CAN FIGHT UNLESS HE IS PROPERLY FED ON BEEF AND BEER.

JOHN CHURCHILL

Quaintest thoughts
– queerest fancies
Come to life and fade away;
What care I how time advances?
I am drinking ale today.

EDGAR ALLAN POE

KEEPING ONE'S GUESTS SUPPLIED WITH LIQUOR IS THE FIRST LAW OF HOSPITALITY.

MARGARET WAY

The church is near,
but the road is icy.
The bar is far, but I
will walk carefully.

RUSSIAN PROVERB

GOD MADE
YEAST, AS WELL
AS DOUGH,
AND LOVES
FERMENTATION
JUST AS DEARLY
AS HE LOVES
VEGETATION.

RALPH WALDO EMERSON

WHEN I READ
ABOUT THE
EVILS OF
DRINKING,
I GAVE UP
READING.

HENNY YOUNGMAN

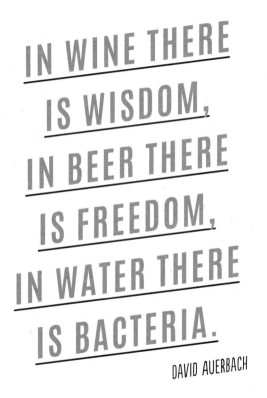

IN WINE THERE IS WISDOM, IN BEER THERE IS FREEDOM, IN WATER THERE IS BACTERIA.

DAVID AUERBACH

IF THIS DOG
DO YOU BITE,
SOON AS OUT
OF YOUR BED,
TAKE A HAIR OF
THE TAIL IN THE
MORNING.

SCOTTISH PROVERB

A DRINK A DAY KEEPS THE SHRINK AWAY.

EDWARD ABBEY

MEET ME DOWN IN THE BAR! WE'LL DRINK BREAKFAST TOGETHER.

W. C. FIELDS

Sometimes too much to drink is barely enough.

Mark Twain

—

ALCOHOL, TAKEN
IN SUFFICIENT
QUANTITIES, MAY
PRODUCE ALL
THE EFFECTS OF
DRUNKENNESS.

—

OSCAR WILDE

NEVER TRUST A MAN who DOESN'T DRINK.

JAMES CRUMLEY

I drink when I have occasion, and sometimes when I have no occasion.

MIGUEL DE CERVANTES

THE MOUTH OF A PERFECTLY HAPPY MAN IS FILLED WITH BEER.

ANCIENT EGYPTIAN PROVERB

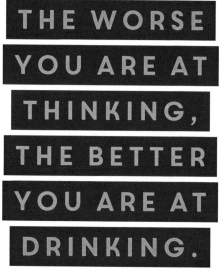

THE WORSE YOU ARE AT THINKING, THE BETTER YOU ARE AT DRINKING.

TERRY GOODKIND

BUT I'M NOT SO THINK AS YOU DRUNK I AM.

J. C. SQUIRE

Let a man walk ten miles
steadily on a hot summer's
day along a dusty English road,
and he will soon discover
why beer was invented.

G. K. CHESTERTON

ALE, MAN,
ALE'S THE STUFF
TO DRINK
FOR FELLOWS
WHOM IT HURTS
TO THINK.

A. E. HOUSMAN

WHEN
I'M DRUNK,
I BITE.

BETTE MIDLER

DRINK IS
THE FEAST OF
REASON AND THE
FLOW OF SOUL.

ALEXANDER POPE

SOBER OR BLOTTO, THIS IS YOUR MOTTO: KEEP MUDDLING THROUGH.

P. G. WODEHOUSE

THE PROBLEM WITH THE WORLD IS THAT EVERYONE IS A FEW DRINKS BEHIND.

HUMPHREY BOGART

I HAVE TAKEN
MORE OUT OF
ALCOHOL THAN
ALCOHOL HAS
TAKEN OUT
OF ME.

WINSTON CHURCHILL

It takes only one drink to get me drunk. The trouble is, I can't remember if it's the thirteenth or the fourteenth.

GEORGE BURNS

ABSTAINER:
A WEAK PERSON
WHO YIELDS TO
THE TEMPTATION
OF DENYING
HIMSELF A
PLEASURE.

AMBROSE BIERCE

Drink what you want; drink what you're able. If you are drinking with me, you'll be under the table.

ANONYMOUS

—

MAY YOUR GLASS BE
EVER FULL, MAY THE
ROOF OVER YOUR HEAD
BE ALWAYS STRONG,
AND MAY YOU BE IN
HEAVEN HALF AN HOUR
BEFORE THE DEVIL
KNOWS YOU'RE DEAD.

—

IRISH TOAST

DRINKING
IS A WAY
— *of* —
ENDING
THE DAY.

ERNEST HEMINGWAY

What harm in drinking
can there be,
Since punch and life
so well agree?

THOMAS BLACKLOCK

HEALTH —
WHAT MY
FRIENDS
ARE ALWAYS
DRINKING TO
BEFORE THEY
FALL DOWN.

PHYLLIS DILLER

MAN, BEING REASONABLE, MUST GET DRUNK; THE BEST OF LIFE IS BUT INTOXICATION.

LORD BYRON

YOU HAVE
TO DRINK,
OTHERWISE
YOU'D GO STARK
STARING SOBER.

KEITH WATERHOUSE

Alcohol is a
misunderstood
vitamin.

P. G. WODEHOUSE

WOMAN FIRST
TEMPTED MAN TO
EAT; HE TOOK TO
DRINKING OF HIS
OWN ACCORD.

JOHN R. KEMBLE

IF I HAD TO LIVE MY LIFE OVER, I'D LIVE OVER A SALOON.

W. C. FIELDS

TOPPING BEER OFF WITH WINE – THAT'S FINE!

GERMAN PROVERB

WHAT'S DRINKING? A MERE PAUSE FROM THINKING!

LORD BYRON

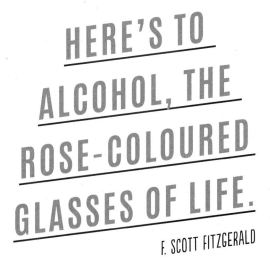

HERE'S TO ALCOHOL, THE ROSE-COLOURED GLASSES OF LIFE.

F. SCOTT FITZGERALD

MILK IS FOR BABIES. WHEN YOU GROW UP YOU HAVE TO DRINK BEER.

ARNOLD SCHWARZENEGGER

WHAT TWO IDEAS ARE MORE INSEPARABLE THAN BEER AND BRITANNIA?

SYDNEY SMITH

Beauty is in the eye of the beer holder.

Kinky Friedman

—

YOU CAN'T
BE A REAL
COUNTRY UNLESS
YOU HAVE A BEER
AND AN AIRLINE.

—

FRANK ZAPPA

BEER,
IT'S THE
BEST
— *damn* —
DRINK
IN THE WORLD.

JACK NICHOLSON

There is no such thing as a bad beer. It's that some taste better than others.

BILLY CARTER

I'M GAINING WEIGHT THE RIGHT WAY: I'M DRINKING BEER.

JOHNNY DAMON

Not all chemicals are bad.
Without chemicals such as
hydrogen and oxygen, for
example, there would be no
way to make water, a vital
ingredient in beer.

DAVE BARRY

ALCOHOL IS NOT
THE ANSWER;
IT JUST MAKES
YOU FORGET THE
QUESTION.

ANONYMOUS

There's alcohol
in plant and tree.
It must be Nature's plan
That there should be
in fair degree
Some alcohol in Man.

A. P. HERBERT

AH, DRINK
AGAIN THIS
RIVER THAT IS
THE TAKER-AWAY
OF PAIN, AND
THE GIVER-BACK
OF BEAUTY!

EDNA ST. VINCENT MILLAY

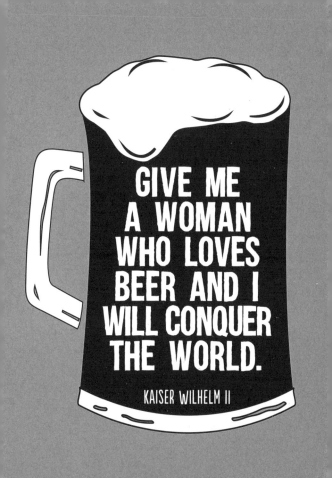

GIVE ME
A WOMAN
WHO LOVES
BEER AND I
WILL CONQUER
THE WORLD.

KAISER WILHELM II

THE DIFFERENCE
BETWEEN A
DRUNK AND AN
ALCOHOLIC IS
THAT A DRUNK
DOESN'T HAVE
TO ATTEND ALL
THOSE MEETINGS.

W. ARTHUR LEWIS

NO ANIMAL
EVER INVENTED
ANYTHING
SO BAD AS
DRUNKENNESS –
OR SO GOOD
AS DRINK.

G. K. CHESTERTON

BEER MAKES YOU FEEL THE WAY YOU OUGHT TO FEEL WITHOUT BEER.

HENRY LAWSON

ALCOHOL
MAY BE MAN'S
WORST ENEMY,
BUT THE BIBLE
SAYS LOVE
YOUR ENEMY.

FRANK SINATRA

I'VE NEVER BEEN THROWN OUT OF A PUB, BUT I'VE FALLEN INTO QUITE A FEW.

BENNY BELLAMACINA

For a quart of Ale is a dish for a king.

William Shakespeare

—

BEER, IF DRUNK IN
MODERATION, SOFTENS
THE TEMPER, CHEERS
THE SPIRIT AND
PROMOTES HEALTH.

—

THOMAS JEFFERSON

A MAN
WHO LIES ABOUT
BEER
— makes —
ENEMIES.

STEPHEN KING

Teetotallers lack the sympathy and generosity of men that drink.

W. H. DAVIES

WITHOUT QUESTION, THE GREATEST INVENTION IN THE HISTORY OF MANKIND IS BEER.

DAVE BARRY

I ONLY TAKE A DRINK ON TWO OCCASIONS – WHEN I'M THIRSTY AND WHEN I'M NOT.

BRENDAN BEHAN

A MAN OUGHT TO GET DRUNK AT LEAST TWICE A YEAR... SO HE WON'T LET HIMSELF GET SNOTTY ABOUT IT.

RAYMOND CHANDLER

You're not drunk
if you can lie on
the floor without
holding on.

DEAN MARTIN

A WOMAN DROVE ME TO DRINK AND I DIDN'T EVEN HAVE THE DECENCY TO THANK HER.

W. C. FIELDS

Always do sober what
you said you'd do drunk.
That will teach you to keep
your mouth shut.

ERNEST HEMINGWAY

TWENTY-FOUR HOURS IN A DAY, TWENTY-FOUR BEERS IN A CASE. COINCIDENCE?

STEVEN WRIGHT

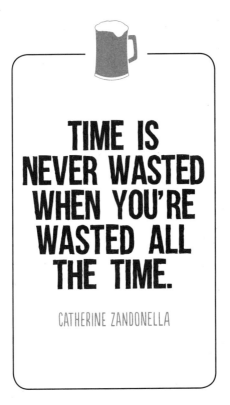

TIME IS
NEVER WASTED
WHEN YOU'RE
WASTED ALL
THE TIME.

CATHERINE ZANDONELLA

A FINE BEER MAY BE JUDGED WITH ONLY ONE SIP, BUT IT'S BETTER TO BE THOROUGHLY SURE.

CZECH PROVERB

I FEAR THE MAN WHO DRINKS WATER AND SO REMEMBERS THIS MORNING WHAT THE REST OF US SAID LAST NIGHT.

GREEK PROVERB

BEER... A HIGH AND MIGHTY LIQUOR.

JULIUS CAESAR

A MAN CAN HIDE ALL THINGS, EXCEPTING TWAIN - THAT HE IS DRUNK, AND THAT HE IS IN LOVE.

ANTIPHANES

'Ere's to English women an' a quart of English beer.

Rudyard Kipling

GIVE MY PEOPLE
PLENTY OF BEER, GOOD
BEER, AND CHEAP
BEER, AND YOU WILL
HAVE NO REVOLUTION
AMONG THEM.

QUEEN VICTORIA

IT TAKES

BEER

TO MAKE

— thirst —

WORTHWHILE.

GERMAN PROVERB

If you ever reach
total enlightenment while
drinking beer, I bet it makes
beer shoot out your nose.

JACK HANDEY

NO POEMS CAN LIVE LONG OR PLEASE THAT ARE WRITTEN BY WATER-DRINKERS.

HORACE

TOO MUCH
WORK AND NO
VACATION,
DESERVES
AT LEAST
A SMALL
LIBATION.

OSCAR WILDE

HE THAT DRINKETH STRONG BEER AND GOES TO BED RIGHT MELLOW, LIVES AS HE OUGHT TO LIVE AND DIES A HEARTY FELLOW.

TRADITIONAL TOAST

He is not deserving the name
of Englishman who speaketh
against ale, that is, good ale.

GEORGE BORROW

ALCOHOL MAY
NOT SOLVE YOUR
PROBLEMS, BUT
NEITHER WILL
WATER OR MILK.

ANONYMOUS

I NEVER MET A PUB I DIDN'T LIKE.

PETE SLOSBERG

BEER NEEDS BASEBALL, AND BASEBALL NEEDS BEER – IT HAS ALWAYS BEEN THUS.

PETER RICHMOND

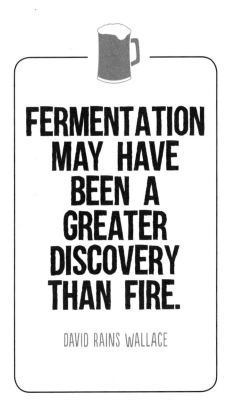

FERMENTATION MAY HAVE BEEN A GREATER DISCOVERY THAN FIRE.

DAVID RAINS WALLACE

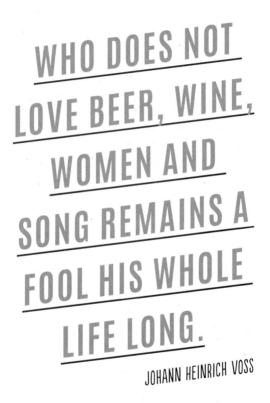

WHO DOES NOT LOVE BEER, WINE, WOMEN AND SONG REMAINS A FOOL HIS WHOLE LIFE LONG.

JOHANN HEINRICH VOSS

I ENVY PEOPLE
WHO DRINK –
AT LEAST THEY
KNOW WHAT
TO BLAME
EVERYTHING ON.

OSCAR LEVANT

I WOULD GIVE ALL MY FAME FOR A POT OF ALE, AND SAFETY.

WILLIAM SHAKESPEARE

OH, YOU HATE YOUR JOB?...
THERE'S A SUPPORT GROUP FOR THAT.
IT'S CALLED *EVERYBODY*, AND
THEY MEET AT THE BAR.

DREW CAREY

Drink because you are happy, but never because you are miserable.

G. K. Chesterton

—

NINETY-NINE
PER CENT OF ALL
PROBLEMS CAN BE
SOLVED BY MONEY -
AND FOR THE OTHER
ONE PER CENT
THERE'S ALCOHOL.

—

QUENTIN R. BUFOGLE

THOSE
WHO DRINK
BEER
— *will* —
THINK
BEER.

WASHINGTON IRVING

Ignorance is a lot like alcohol: the more you have of it, the less you are able to see its effect on you.

JAY M. BYLSMA

I'M A
DRINKER
WITH
WRITING
PROBLEMS.

BRENDAN BEHAN

When you stop drinking,
you have to deal with this
marvellous personality that
started you drinking in
the first place.

JIMMY BRESLIN

I NEVER DRINK WHILE I'M WORKING, BUT AFTER A FEW GLASSES I GET IDEAS THAT WOULD NEVER HAVE OCCURRED TO ME DEAD SOBER.

IRWIN SHAW

The only cure
for a real hangover
is death.

ROBERT BENCHLEY

I HAVE FED
PURELY UPON
ALE; I HAVE EAT
MY ALE, DRANK
MY ALE, AND I
ALWAYS SLEEP
UPON ALE.

GEORGE FARQUHAR

ONE MORE
DRINK AND
I'D HAVE
BEEN UNDER
THE HOST!

DOROTHY PARKER

ALCOHOL IS LIKE
LOVE. THE FIRST
KISS IS MAGIC,
THE SECOND
IS INTIMATE,
THE THIRD
IS ROUTINE.

RAYMOND CHANDLER

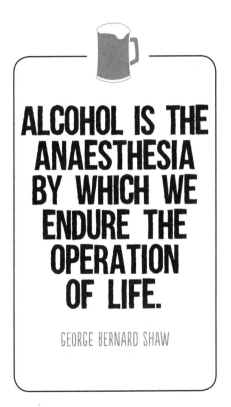

ALCOHOL IS THE ANAESTHESIA BY WHICH WE ENDURE THE OPERATION OF LIFE.

GEORGE BERNARD SHAW

THE WORST THING ABOUT SOME MEN IS THAT WHEN THEY ARE NOT DRUNK THEY ARE SOBER.

WILLIAM BUTLER YEATS

EVEN THOUGH A NUMBER OF PEOPLE HAVE TRIED, NO ONE HAS YET FOUND A WAY TO DRINK FOR A LIVING.

JEAN KERR

BACCHUS, N.
A CONVENIENT
DEITY INVENTED
BY THE ANCIENTS
AS AN EXCUSE FOR
GETTING DRUNK.

AMBROSE BIERCE

I drink
exactly as much
as I want, and one
drink more.

H. L. Mencken

—

ALCOHOL IS
NECESSARY FOR
A MAN SO THAT HE
CAN HAVE A GOOD
OPINION OF HIMSELF,
UNDISTURBED BY
THE FACTS.

—

FINLEY PETER DUNNE

THE
DRUNK MIND
SPEAKS
— the —
SOBER
HEART.

ANONYMOUS

Know thyself, especially
thyself after a couple
of drinks.

ROBERT BRAULT

DRUNKENNESS IS NOTHING BUT VOLUNTARY MADNESS.

SENECA THE YOUNGER

DRINK THE FIRST. SIP THE SECOND SLOWLY. SKIP THE THIRD.

KNUTE ROCKNE

NOTHING GIVES A SENSATION BETTER THAN A BEER! NOTHING BUILDS A RELATION BETTER THAN A BEER!

ANSHUL DUBEY

My grandmother
is over 80 and
still doesn't need
glasses. Drinks right
out of the bottle.

HENNY YOUNGMAN

I DISTRUST CAMELS, AND ANYONE ELSE WHO CAN GO A WEEK WITHOUT A DRINK.

JOE E. LEWIS

A LITTLE
BIT OF BEER
IS DIVINE
MEDICINE.

PARACELSUS

MOST PEOPLE
HATE THE TASTE
OF BEER TO
BEGIN WITH. IT
IS, HOWEVER, A
PREJUDICE THAT
MANY PEOPLE
HAVE BEEN ABLE
TO OVERCOME.

WINSTON CHURCHILL

On some days, my head is
filled with such wild and
original thoughts that I can
barely utter a word. On other
days the liquor store is closed.

FRANK VARANO

FISHING, WITH ME, HAS ALWAYS BEEN AN EXCUSE TO DRINK IN THE DAYTIME.

JIMMY CANNON

THE BEST WAY
TO JUDGE A
PUB IS BY THE
ALBUMS ON ITS
JUKEBOX.

NED BEAUMAN

By the time a bartender
knows what drink a man
will have before he orders,
there is little else about
him worth knowing.

DON MARQUIS

BUT IF AT CHURCH
THEY WOULD GIVE
US SOME ALE...
WE'D SING AND
WE'D PRAY ALL
THE LIVE-LONG DAY.

WILLIAM BLAKE

Did your
mother never tell
you not to drink on
an empty head?

Billy Connolly

—

WHEN YOU'RE THIRSTY
AND IT SEEMS THAT
YOU COULD DRINK THE
ENTIRE OCEAN, THAT'S
FAITH; WHEN YOU START
TO DRINK AND FINISH
ONLY A GLASS OR TWO,
THAT'S SCIENCE.

—

ANTON CHEKHOV

OF COURSE
ONE SHOULD
NOT DRINK
— *much.* —
BUT OFTEN.

HENRI DE TOULOUSE-LAUTREC

Drink not the third glass,
which thou canst not tame,
when once it is within thee.

GEORGE HERBERT

IT IS NOT HOW MUCH WE HAVE, BUT HOW MUCH WE ENJOY, THAT MAKES HAPPINESS.

CHARLES SPURGEON

SIMPLY ENJOY LIFE AND THE GREAT PLEASURES THAT COME WITH IT.

KAROLINA KURKOVA

I HAVE A
THEORY THAT
THE SECRET
OF MARITAL
HAPPINESS IS
SIMPLE: DRINK
IN DIFFERENT
PUBS TO YOUR
OTHER HALF.

JILLY COOPER

Love makes the
world go round?
Not at all. Whisky
makes it go round
twice as fast.

COMPTON MACKENZIE

THERE IS NOTHING FOR A CASE OF NERVES LIKE A CASE OF BEER.

JOAN GOLDSTEIN

BEER
SPEAKS.
PEOPLE
MUMBLE.

TONY MAGEE

BEER IS
NOT A GOOD
COCKTAIL-
PARTY DRINK,
ESPECIALLY IN
A HOME WHERE
YOU DON'T KNOW
WHERE THE
BATHROOM IS.

BILLY CARTER

THE PUB IS THE INTERNET. IT'S WHERE INFORMATION IS GATHERED, COLLATED AND ADDRESSED.

RHYS IFANS

BEER... AN INTOXICATING GOLDEN BREW THAT RE-EMERGES VIRTUALLY UNCHANGED AN HOUR LATER.

RICK BAYAN

I'M NOT
A HEAVY
DRINKER.
I CAN
SOMETIMES
GO FOR HOURS
WITHOUT
TOUCHING
A DROP.

NOËL COWARD

How much of our
literature, our political life,
our friendships and love
affairs, depend on being able
to talk peacefully in a bar!

JOHN WAIN

THERE IS NOTHING WHICH HAS BEEN YET CONTRIVED BY MAN, BY WHICH SO MUCH HAPPINESS IS PRODUCED AS BY A GOOD TAVERN OR INN.

SAMUEL JOHNSON

SHOULDER THE SKY,

MY LAD,

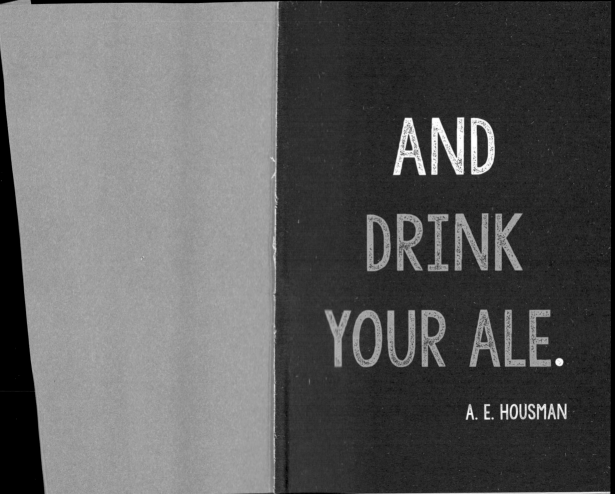

If you're interested in finding out more about our books, find us on Facebook at Summersdale Publishers and follow us on Twitter at @Summersdale.

www.summersdale.com